PROSPERITY PLAYBOOK:

Mastering Wealth Creation & Management For The Modern Investor

Alexandre Smith

CONTENTS

1. INTRODUCTION: THE JOURNEY TO PROSPERITY

Welcome to the beginning of your transformative journey towards prosperity. In this chapter, we will delve even deeper into key concepts, strategies, and mindsets that can help you create wealth and financial abundance. Whether you're just starting your career, running your own business, or managing your personal finances, this guide will provide you with the tools and insights to pave the way for a prosperous future.

Defining Prosperity: Unveiling the True Meaning of Financial Success

To embark on this transformative journey towards prosperity, it is essential to understand what prosperity truly means to you. While many view it purely from a financial lens, it encompasses much more than the accumulation of wealth. True prosperity involves achieving a state of holistic well-being and fulfillment across various areas of your life, including relationships, health, personal growth, and contribution to society. Taking a moment to reflect on what prosperity means to you personally will serve as the guiding star throughout this journey, ensuring that your pursuit of wealth aligns with your core values and aspirations.

The Power of Financial Literacy: Building a Strong Foundation

In the pursuit of prosperity, financial literacy becomes the cornerstone on which you build a strong foundation. It is the ability to understand and effectively manage your money, enabling you to make informed decisions that align with your financial goals. Enhancing your financial literacy involves educating yourself on key concepts such as budgeting, saving, investing, debt management, and risk mitigation. By developing this knowledge, you gain the confidence and competence to navigate the complex world of personal finance, allowing you to maximize your wealth-building potential.

Navigating the Entrepreneurial Mindset: Unlocking Opportunities for Wealth Creation

Beyond financial literacy, adopting an entrepreneurial mindset is crucial for unlocking opportunities that lead to wealth creation. An entrepreneurial mindset is characterized by attributes such as creativity, resilience, problem-solving, and a willingness to embrace calculated risks. Cultivating this mindset enables you to identify and seize opportunities for growth and success, whether as a business owner or within a larger organization. It encourages you to think critically, challenge conventional wisdom, and constantly seek innovative solutions. By embracing an entrepreneurial mindset, you can navigate the ever changing landscape of the modern economy, adapt to new challenges, and turn obstacles into stepping stones towards prosperity.

Investment Strategies:

Building Wealth through Smart and Informed Choices

Once you have established a solid foundation of financial literacy and an entrepreneurial mindset, it is time to explore investment strategies that can propel your journey towards prosperity. Investments are essential vehicles for wealth creation, providing a means to grow and protect your hard-earned money. Building an investment portfolio requires a deep understanding of risk and return, asset allocation, diversification, and the ability to adapt to market conditions. By conducting thorough research, seeking professional advice, and continuously monitoring and adjusting your investments, you can make informed decisions that align with your financial goals and risk tolerance.

Learning from Success Stories:

Insights from Remarkable Achievers

Throughout this journey towards prosperity, drawing inspiration from success stories can provide practical insights and lessons that you can apply to your own unique circumstances. Studying individuals and organizations that have achieved remarkable financial success allows you to gain valuable insights into their mindset, strategies, and decision-making processes. By analyzing their paths to prosperity, you can learn from their achievements, avoid common pitfalls, and accelerate your progress. Successful individuals often emphasize the importance of continuous learning, adaptability, perseverance, and the ability to leverage strengths and seize opportunities. By incorporating these lessons into your own journey, you can navigate challenges with greater confidence and achieve your desired level of prosperity.

Personal Development:

Nurturing Traits and Skills for Success

In the pursuit of financial success, personal development plays a pivotal role. Cultivating a positive mindset, enhancing your productivity and efficiency, and fostering a growth-oriented attitude are essential for long-term prosperity. Continuous learning and acquiring new knowledge are crucial to staying ahead in a rapidly evolving world. Investing in your skillset, both technical and soft, allows you to adapt to changing market demands and excel in your chosen field. Networking and building strong relationships provide access to opportunities, mentorship, knowledge, and support. Taking care of your physical and mental well-being ensures you have the energy, focus, and resilience needed to navigate challenges and seize opportunities effectively.

Creating a Life of Abundance, Fulfillment, and Impact

As we embark on this transformative journey, it's crucial to remember that prosperity is not solely about accumulating wealth. It is about creating a life of abundance, fulfillment, and impact. Aligning your financial goals with your passions and values will enable you to forge a path that is both financially rewarding and personally meaningful. Seek ways to give back to your community and make a positive impact on the lives of others, whether through charitable endeavors, mentorship, or socially responsible investments. By equipping yourself with knowledge, adopting an entrepreneurial mindset, and making smart financial decisions, you are setting the stage for a prosperous future filled with purpose and joy.

Conclusion

Now armed with a deeper understanding of the journey towards prosperity, you are primed to take the next steps. Commit yourself to continuous learning, embrace an entrepreneurial mindset, and make informed financial decisions. By doing so, you will unlock your fullest potential and set yourself on the path towards a life of abundance and impact. Remember, this is just the beginning of an incredible journey, and the possibilities for your financial success and personal fulfillment are limitless. Let us embark on this transformative journey together, as we unveil the pathway to prosperity and create a life of abundance, fulfillment, and impact.

Prosperity Playbook: Mastering Wealth Creation
& Management For The Modern Investor

———————

2. THE POWER OF FINANCIAL LITERACY

Knowledge is power, and when it comes to finances, this statement couldn't be more accurate. Without a solid understanding of the principles of personal finance, it can be challenging to navigate the complex world of money management and wealth creation. In this chapter, we will explore the importance of financial literacy and how it can positively impact your journey to prosperity.

Financial literacy refers to the ability to understand and effectively use various financial skills, including budgeting, saving, investing, and managing debt. It is a crucial life skill that empowers individuals to make informed decisions about their money, ensuring long-term financial stability and success. Unfortunately, many people lack the necessary knowledge and skills to handle their finances effectively.

The first step toward improving financial literacy is to develop a basic understanding of financial concepts and terms. This includes learning about budgeting and the importance of tracking expenses accurately. A budget is a roadmap that helps you allocate your income effectively, ensuring that you are not overspending and are saving enough for future needs. It allows you to prioritize your financial goals and make conscious choices about where your money goes. Tracking expenses not only helps you stick to your budget but also allows you to see where your money is going, enabling you to identify opportunities for saving.

Furthermore, understanding different types of savings accounts and investments is essential in building a solid financial foundation. Savings accounts provide a safe place to store your money while earning some interest. However, not all savings accounts are created equal. It is crucial to compare interest rates and fees among different banks to maximize your savings. There are also various types of investment opportunities with different risk and return profiles. Acquiring knowledge about different investment options, such as stocks, bonds, mutual funds, and real estate, allows you to make informed decisions based on your risk tolerance and financial goals.

Another key aspect of financial literacy is understanding the impact of financial decisions on your overall financial well-being. By analyzing your spending patterns, you can identify areas where you can cut back on unnecessary expenses. This, in turn, allows you to redirect those funds toward savings and investments. Developing good financial habits, such as distinguishing between needs and wants, practicing delayed gratification, and avoiding impulsive purchases, can significantly impact your ability to save and invest for the future. By practicing discipline and making intentional choices about your spending, you can avoid falling into the trap of living beyond your means and accumulating debt.

Speaking of debt, it is crucial to comprehend the role of credit and how to manage it wisely. Credit can be a useful tool for achieving financial goals, such as purchasing a home or starting a business. However, it is essential to use credit responsibly and understand the consequences of borrowing money. Understanding interest rates, credit scores, and the impact of missed payments can help you manage your debts effectively and protect your financial health. Developing a strategy to pay off high-interest debts and avoiding unnecessary borrowing can contribute significantly to your overall financial well-being.

Furthermore, financial literacy encompasses the ability to evaluate investment opportunities and assess their potential risks and rewards. This understanding allows you to make informed decisions about where to allocate your money. For instance, the stock market offers the potential for significant returns. However, it also comes with fluctuations and uncertainties. Learning about diversification and the importance of spreading your investments across different asset classes can mitigate risks and optimize your returns. Additionally, understanding the concept of compounding returns can help you make the most of your investments by allowing your money to grow over time.

Lastly, financial literacy involves staying informed about current economic trends and understanding how they can impact your financial situation. Keeping an eye on market developments and continuously educating yourself about financial matters helps you adapt your financial strategy to changing circumstances. By understanding the relationship between economic indicators, such as inflation rates, interest rates, and employment data, you can make more informed decisions about investments, debt management, and financial planning. Being proactive and continuously seeking knowledge about personal finance ensures that you are equipped to make sound financial decisions throughout your life.

In conclusion, the power of financial literacy cannot be overstated. By arming yourself with knowledge and skills in personal finance, you can take control of your financial future and make sound decisions that lead to long-term prosperity. It is an essential skill set that empowers individuals to create wealth, manage resources effectively, and achieve their financial goals. Embrace the power of financial literacy, and watch as it transforms your journey to prosperity.

____

3. THE ENTREPRENEURIAL MINDSET

In order to achieve financial prosperity, it is essential to adopt an entrepreneurial mindset. This mindset goes beyond simply starting a business; it is a way of thinking and approaching life that can lead to great success.

The entrepreneurial mindset is characterized by traits such as ambition, innovation, resilience, and a willingness to take risks. It involves seeing opportunities where others see obstacles and embracing challenges as learning opportunities.

One of the key aspects of the entrepreneurial mindset is the ability to identify and seize opportunities. Entrepreneurs have a keen sense of observation, constantly scanning the environment for potential business ideas or gaps in the market. They possess the ability to envision possibilities and connect the dots, leveraging their creativity and imagination to develop innovative solutions. This mindset encourages individuals to think outside the box and challenge the status quo.

To cultivate this mindset, individuals can practice actively seeking out new experiences and perspectives. They can explore different industries, network with diverse individuals, and engage in continuous learning opportunities. By expanding their knowledge and understanding of various sectors, they become better equipped to identify untapped opportunities and develop unique business concepts.

Moreover, to seize opportunities effectively, entrepreneurs need to remain open and adaptable to change. They understand that the market is constantly evolving, and consumer preferences and technologies are continually shifting. By staying agile and responsive to these changes, entrepreneurs can pivot their business strategies as needed and stay ahead of the curve. This flexibility requires a willingness to let go of attachment to one particular idea or approach, instead embracing a mindset of continuous learning and adaptation.

Another important aspect of the entrepreneurial mindset is resilience. Starting and running a business is not a linear path, and setbacks and failures are bound to happen along the way.

However, entrepreneurs view these setbacks as temporary obstacles and find ways to overcome them. They have the mental fortitude to handle adversity, embracing it as an opportunity for growth and learning.

Resilience can be nurtured by cultivating a growth mindset, which is the belief that intelligence and abilities can be developed through dedication and hard work. Entrepreneurs with a growth mindset view challenges as opportunities to expand their skills and knowledge. They embrace failure as a stepping stone towards success, analyzing what went wrong, and using those lessons to improve future outcomes.

In addition to resilience, risk-taking is also a significant part of the entrepreneurial mindset. Entrepreneurs understand that taking calculated risks is necessary for growth and success. They carefully assess the potential rewards and consequences of each decision, weighing the possibilities and making informed choices. Risk-taking requires courage, intuition, and the ability to trust one's instincts.

However, it is important to note that risk-taking does not mean reckless behavior. Entrepreneurs analyze and manage risk by conducting thorough research, developing contingency plans, and seeking advice from trusted mentors or industry experts. They understand that taking calculated risks involves balancing potential gains with potential losses and making informed decisions based on careful evaluation.

Furthermore, the entrepreneurial mindset embraces innovation. Entrepreneurs are not content with the status quo; they constantly seek new and better ways to solve problems and meet the needs of the market. They cultivate a culture of creative thinking, encouraging their team members to contribute their unique perspectives and harnessing the power of collaboration. Entrepreneurs understand that innovation is crucial for staying competitive and driving growth.

To foster an innovative mindset, individuals can practice being curious and open-minded. This involves questioning existing assumptions, challenging conventional wisdom, and exploring new possibilities. Entrepreneurs actively seek out opportunities for learning and growth, attending industry conferences, participating in workshops, and engaging in continuous professional development.

Entrepreneurs also embrace the concept of failing fast and failing forward. This means rapidly testing ideas, prototypes, and minimum viable products in the market to gather feedback and make necessary improvements. Rather than fearing failure, entrepreneurs view it as an integral part of

the innovation process. By embracing failure as a learning opportunity, entrepreneurs can refine their products and services, ultimately increasing their
chances of success.

Developing an entrepreneurial mindset is not limited to aspiring business owners. It can benefit anyone looking to achieve financial prosperity. This mindset encourages individuals to think creatively, take risks, persevere through challenges, and continuously strive for improvement. It enables individuals to identify opportunities, make sound decisions, and adapt to changing circumstances.

In conclusion, the entrepreneurial mindset is a powerful tool for achieving financial prosperity. It encompasses traits such as ambition, innovation, resilience, and a willingness to take risks. By embracing this mindset, individuals can unlock their potential and seize opportunities that can lead to great success. The journey to financial prosperity requires a mindset that is focused, adaptable, and relentless in pursuing growth and success. It is in harnessing these entrepreneurial traits that individuals can navigate the complexities of the business world and achieve their goals.

---

4. INVESTMENT STRATEGIES 101

Investing can be a daunting task for many individuals, but with proper knowledge and strategies, it can become a powerful tool for wealth creation. In this chapter, we will delve into the basics of investment strategies and explore key principles that can help you navigate the world of investing.

1. Understand Your Goals: Before embarking on any investment journey, it is crucial to define your financial goals. Are you looking for short-term gains or long-term growth? Are you aiming for a stable income stream or capital appreciation? Knowing your goals will guide your investment decisions and help you select the right investment vehicles.

a. Short-Term Goals:

If you have short-term goals, such as saving for a vacation or buying a car, it is advisable to focus on investments that provide liquidity and stability. Consider options like high-yield savings accounts, money market funds, or short-term bonds.

b. Long-Term Goals: Long-term goals, such as retirement planning or funding your children's education, require a different approach. You can afford to take more risks and invest in assets with higher growth potential, such as stocks, real estate, or long-term bonds.

2. Diversification is Key: One of the most important investment strategies is diversification. Diversifying your portfolio by investing in a mix of different asset classes can help spread out the risk and potentially increase your returns. The basic principle behind diversification is that not all investments will perform well at the same time. By not putting all your eggs in one basket, you minimize the impact of a single investment's performance on your overall portfolio. Some commonly used asset classes for diversification include:

a. Stocks: Investing in stocks allows you to participate in the ownership of companies. Stocks can provide growth potential and dividends. It is important to consider factors like company fundamentals, growth potential, and market conditions when selecting stocks. You can choose to invest in individual stocks or opt for exchange-traded funds (ETFs) or mutual funds that provide diversification within a specific market segment or sector.

b. Bonds: Bonds are essentially debt instruments issued by governments, municipalities, and corporations to raise capital. They provide fixed returns and are considered relatively more stable than stocks. Investing in different types of bonds, such as government bonds, corporate bonds, and municipal bonds, can diversify your portfolio and provide a stable income stream. Factors to consider include credit ratings, interest rate environments, and maturity dates.

c. Real Estate: Investing in real estate can be done directly by purchasing properties or indirectly through real estate investment trusts (REITs) or real estate mutual funds. Real estate investments can provide long-term growth potential, rental income, and inflation protection. Factors to consider include property location, market trends, rental demand, and management costs.

d. Commodities: Commodities include assets such as gold, silver, oil, natural gas, and agricultural products. Investing in commodities can provide protection against inflation and diversify your portfolio by including non-traditional assets. Factors to consider include supply and demand dynamics, geopolitical events, and global economic conditions.

e. Alternative Investments: Alternative investments, such as private equity, hedge funds, or venture capital, offer opportunities beyond traditional asset classes. These investments are typically available to accredited investors and come with higher risks and potential rewards. Factors to consider include investment strategies, track records, and associated fees.

3. Risk versus Return: Every investment carries some level of risk. The key is to find a balance between risk and return that aligns with your risk tolerance. Generally, investments with higher potential returns also come with higher risks. It is important to assess your risk appetite and choose investments accordingly. Common risk categories include:

a. Market Risk: Market fluctuations, economic factors, and geopolitical events can affect the performance of your investments. Being aware of potential market risks and diversifying your portfolio can help mitigate their impact. Staying informed about market trends, economic indicators, and industry news is essential.

b. Credit Risk: This refers to the possibility of an issuer defaulting on their debt obligations. Diversifying across issuers with different credit ratings can reduce credit risk. Conducting thorough credit analysis or investing in bond funds managed by professionals can help manage credit risk.

c. Liquidity Risk: Liquidity risk refers to the difficulty of selling your assets quickly at fair prices. Investments in less liquid assets, such as real estate or certain bonds, may face liquidity constraints. It is important to consider your investment horizon and liquidity needs when selecting investments.

d. Inflation Risk: Inflation erodes the purchasing power of money over time. Investing in assets that have historically outpaced inflation, such as stocks or real estate, can help preserve and grow your wealth. Considering inflationary pressures and investing in inflation-protected securities or assets can help mitigate inflation risk.

4. Time Horizon Matters: Your investment strategy should consider your time horizon. If you have a longer time horizon, you can afford to take more risks and invest in assets with potential long-term growth, such as stocks or real estate. However, if you have a shorter time horizon, you may want to focus on more stable investments, such as bonds or fixed income products, to preserve capital. Time also plays a role in compounding returns. The longer your investment horizon, the more time your investments have to grow and compound.

5. Stay Informed: Knowledge is power when it comes to investing. Stay up-to-date with market trends, economic indicators, and industry news that may impact your investments. Research different investment options, understand their pros and cons, and seek advice from financial experts if needed. The more informed you are, the better equipped you will be to make sound investment decisions.

a. Fundamental Analysis: This involves analyzing a company's financial statements, management team, industry position, and competitive landscape. Fundamental analysis can help you assess the intrinsic value of a stock and make informed investment decisions.

b. Technical Analysis: Technical analysis focuses on studying the historical price and volume data of a security to identify patterns and trends. It helps investors identify entry and exit points based on price patterns, moving averages, and other technical indicators.

c. Economic Analysis: Understanding macroeconomic factors, such as GDP growth rates, inflation, interest rates, and government policies, can provide insights into the overall market and help identify investment opportunities. Keeping track of economic indicators, such as employment reports, consumer sentiment, or central bank actions, can assist in making informed investment decisions.

6. Regular Monitoring and Rebalancing: Investment strategies should not be set in stone. Regularly monitor the performance of your investments and make adjustments as needed. Rebalance your portfolio periodically to ensure that it aligns with your goals and risk profile.

Market conditions change, and so should your investment strategy. Regular review and adjustments can help keep your portfolio on track.

a. Performance Monitoring: Keep track of your investments' performance through regular reviews of financial statements, market news, and performance metrics. Compare your investments' performance to relevant benchmarks. This will help you identify underperforming securities or asset classes and allow you to make informed decisions regarding adjustments to your portfolio.

b. Rebalancing: Over time, some investments may

outperform while others may underperform. This can lead to an imbalance in your portfolio's asset allocation. Rebalancing involves adjusting your portfolio by buying or selling assets to bring it back to its target asset allocation. Rebalancing ensures that your portfolio remains aligned with your goals and risk tolerance. It also allows you to take advantage of market opportunities and mitigate the impact of market fluctuations.

c. Tax Considerations: When rebalancing your portfolio, consider the tax implications of selling investments. Selling investments that have appreciated in value may trigger capital gains tax. You may want to consult with a tax advisor to minimize your tax liabilities and optimize your portfolio.

7. Dollar-Cost Averaging: Dollar-cost averaging is an investment strategy where you invest a fixed amount of money at regular intervals, regardless of market conditions. By consistently investing the same amount, you buy more shares when prices are low and fewer shares when prices are high. This strategy helps reduce the impact of short-term market volatility and can potentially result in better long-term returns. Dollar-cost averaging allows you to take advantage of market fluctuations and accumulate more shares over time.

8. Consider Investment Expenses: When selecting investment vehicles, it is important to consider the associated expenses. Expenses like management fees, commissions, and transaction costs can eat into your returns over time. Compare the expenses of different investment options and consider low-cost alternatives, such as index funds or ETFs, to minimize costs and maximize your returns.

9. Determine your Risk Tolerance: Your risk tolerance is an important factor in determining your investment strategy. Some individuals are comfortable with taking higher risks

and potentially higher returns, while others prefer more conservative investments. Assess your financial situation, investment goals, time horizon, and comfort with market volatility to determine your risk tolerance. Be honest with yourself and make investment decisions that align with your risk tolerance to avoid unnecessary stress or anxiety.

10. Seek Professional Advice: If you are unsure about your investment strategy or lack the time or expertise to manage your investments, consider seeking professional advice. Financial advisors or wealth managers can help assess your goals, risk tolerance, and financial situation to develop a tailored investment strategy. They can also provide guidance on investment selection, portfolio rebalancing, and ongoing monitoring.

Remember, investing is a long-term game and patience is key. Markets may experience fluctuations in the short term, but over time, a well-diversified and carefully managed portfolio has the potential to generate significant returns. By understanding your goals, diversifying your investments, managing risk, staying informed, and regularly reviewing and adjusting your portfolio, you can build a solid investment strategy that aligns with your financial objectives.

5. THE ART OF PRODUCTIVITY AND EFFICIENCY

In today's fast-paced world, productivity and efficiency play pivotal roles in determining success and prosperity. Whether you are an entrepreneur, a professional, or an individual seeking financial freedom, mastering the art of productivity can profoundly impact your journey towards achieving your goals.

Setting Clear Goals: The first step towards improving productivity is to establish clear and measurable goals. Clearly define what you want to achieve, both in the short term and long term. Make sure your goals are specific, achievable, relevant, and time-bound (SMART). Breaking down your goals into smaller, actionable tasks that can be completed within a specific time frame creates a roadmap and provides a clear direction for your efforts.

Prioritization: One of the key aspects of productivity is knowing how to prioritize tasks effectively. Not all tasks hold the same level of importance or urgency. Identifying the tasks that are most important and urgent allows you to allocate your time and energy accordingly. The Eisenhower Matrix is a powerful tool that helps prioritize tasks based on their importance and urgency. By focusing on high-priority tasks, you ensure that you are devoting your efforts to activities that bring the most significant impact towards your goals. Prioritization also helps avoid overwhelm and allows you to make informed decisions about where to invest your resources.

Time Management: Time is a finite resource, and managing it efficiently is crucial for productivity. Develop a schedule or a routine that optimizes your time by allocating specific blocks for different tasks. Avoid falling into the multitasking trap as it can lead to decreased efficiency and quality of work. Instead, focus on one task at a time, leveraging techniques such as time blocking or the Pomodoro Technique to structure your work in manageable intervals. Effective time management involves being mindful of how you allocate, spend, and invest your time. Regularly evaluate how you spend your time by conducting time audits to identify areas where time is being wasted or misallocated.

Eliminating Distractions: In the digital age, distractions are abundant and can significantly hamper productivity. It is necessary to take steps to minimize distractions and create a conducive work environment. Turn off notifications on your phone or computer, minimize social media usage, and establish boundaries to ensure uninterrupted work periods. Consider utilizing productivity tools or apps that help you stay focused and organized, such as time-tracking apps or website blockers. Implementing meditation or mindfulness practices can also enhance your ability to stay present and focused on your tasks. Creating a physical workspace dedicated to work, free from clutter and potential distractions, can also have a positive impact on productivity.

Delegation and Outsourcing: Recognize that you cannot do everything yourself. Delegating tasks that can be handled by others allows you to focus on high-value activities. If possible, consider outsourcing certain tasks or hiring freelancers or employees to lighten your workload. This not only increases efficiency but also frees up time for more critical responsibilities. When delegating, ensure you communicate instructions clearly, provide necessary resources and support, and trust in the capabilities of those you delegate to. Delegation and outsourcing can exponentially increase productivity, as it allows you to leverage others' skills and expertise while focusing on your areas of strength.

Continuous Improvement: Productivity is a skill that can be refined, honed, and improved over time. Your productivity methods and systems should continuously evolve as you gain insight and experience. Stay updated on the latest productivity techniques and tools, and be open to adopting new strategies that enhance your efficiency. Regularly evaluate your progress and make necessary adjustments to optimize your productivity. Look for areas where you can streamline processes, eliminate redundancies, or automate tasks, as these actions can lead to significant productivity gains. Seek feedback from mentors, coaches, or colleagues to gain fresh perspectives and identify blind spots.

Work-Life Balance: While productivity is essential, it should not come at the expense of your well-being and personal life. Strive for a healthy work-life balance that allows you to recharge, connect with loved ones, and pursue hobbies and interests outside of work. Burnout and chronic stress can impair productivity in the long run, so it is crucial to prioritize self-care. Set boundaries around work hours, establish dedicated leisure time, and cultivate healthy habits that support your overall well-being. Regular exercise, proper nutrition, and quality sleep contribute to increased energy levels, mental clarity, and focus, ultimately enhancing productivity both in the short term and long term.

In conclusion, mastering the art of productivity and efficiency is key to maximizing your output, making the most of your

time, and propelling yourself towards prosperity. By setting clear goals, prioritizing tasks, managing time effectively, eliminating distractions, embracing delegation, seeking continuous improvement, and maintaining a healthy work-life balance, you can unlock your full potential and achieve remarkable success. Embrace the art of
productivity, and it will become a powerful tool on your journey to prosperity and fulfillment.

PROSPERITY PLAYBOOK: MASTERING WEALTH CREATION
& MANAGEMENT FOR THE MODERN INVESTOR

---

6. CASE STUDY: SUCCESS STORIES FROM NGOS

In this chapter, we will delve deeper into some inspiring success stories from NGOs (Non Governmental Organizations) that have played a significant role in creating prosperity for individuals and communities. These organizations have been at the forefront of addressing social issues, promoting sustainable development, and uplifting the lives of those in need.

NGOs have emerged as powerful agents of change, working tirelessly to tackle various challenges such as poverty, education, healthcare, clean water, and environmental conservation. Through their efforts, they have brought hope and crucial support to communities around the world. Let's explore some remarkable success stories that highlight the impact these organizations have had on society and how they have contributed to overall prosperity.

1. The Smile Foundation:

The Smile Foundation, an Indian NGO, has been a trailblazer in improving the lives of underprivileged children. With a focus on education and healthcare, the foundation has established numerous initiatives that have positively impacted thousands of young lives. Through their "Mission Education" program, they ensure access to quality education for children from disadvantaged backgrounds. They provide educational support, including scholarships, for children to complete their schooling and vocational training programs to facilitate skill development. Additionally, their "Mobile Hospital Program" ensures healthcare services reach remote areas, providing essential medical care to those who need it most. The foundation equips and operates mobile hospitals, reaching communities with limited access to healthcare facilities, and providing free medical consultations, medicines, and diagnostic services. The Smile Foundation's success lies in its holistic approach, collaborating with local communities to address their specific needs and empowering them to create sustainable change.

2. Grameen Bank:

Grameen Bank is a microfinance organization founded by Nobel laureate Muhammad Yunus in Bangladesh. Adopting a unique approach, the bank offers small loans, particularly to women entrepreneurs who lack access to traditional banking services. Through this microfinance model, Grameen Bank has played a pivotal role in helping individuals lift themselves out of poverty by starting or expanding their businesses. The bank extends credit to borrowers through the concept of solidarity groups, where five individuals come together and act as mutual guarantors for each other's loans, fostering a sense of accountability and support within the community. By promoting financial inclusion and providing access to credit, Grameen Bank has empowered countless individuals, especially women, to achieve economic independence, thereby contributing to their overall prosperity.

3. The Nature Conservancy:

The Nature Conservancy is an international NGO committed to protecting and conserving the Earth's natural resources. Recognizing the urgent need for environmental preservation, the organization has spearheaded impactful initiatives to preserve critical ecosystems and promote sustainable development. By partnering with local communities, governments, and businesses, The Nature Conservancy has successfully protected millions of acres of land and restored vital habitats. These efforts have not only safeguarded biodiversity but also have far-reaching benefits for communities. For example, their work in protecting and restoring coral reefs has not only preserved marine life but has also provided economic opportunities for coastal communities through sustainable tourism and fishing practices. Similarly, their approach to watershed protection has ensured a reliable water supply for communities, supporting agriculture, livelihoods, and overall well-being. The Nature Conservancy has demonstrated that when nature is protected, it can lead to economic stability, job creation, and long-term well-being for communities.

4. BRAC (Bangladesh Rural Advancement Committee):

BRAC, the largest NGO in Bangladesh, has been a driving force in poverty alleviation and social development. Operating in various sectors, including education, healthcare, microfinance, and women's empowerment, BRAC has implemented comprehensive programs to address the multifaceted challenges faced by marginalized communities. Their education programs have improved access to quality schooling, while their healthcare initiatives have provided essential services and improved healthcare outcomes. In addition to primary and secondary education, BRAC has established education centers for out-of school children and accelerated learning programs for older students. Their healthcare programs offer a range of services, from maternal and child healthcare to clinics providing diagnosis and treatment for common illnesses. BRAC's microfinance programs have enabled aspiring entrepreneurs to access credit, start businesses, and break the cycle of poverty. They have established village-based credit groups, providing financial services to people who are often excluded from traditional banking systems. Additionally, their women empowerment programs have empowered women in leadership positions, promoting gender equality and fostering sustainable development. BRAC's initiatives include skills training, income-generating activities, and platforms for women's voices to be heard in decision-making processes. The collective impact of these integrated programs has transformed the lives of millions and created a path to sustainable prosperity.

These success stories from NGOs highlight the immense potential for positive change and prosperity that these organizations possess. By showcasing their innovative approaches, collaborative efforts, and transformative outcomes, we aim to inspire individuals, communities, and policymakers to support and replicate their strategies. It is through the collective efforts of NGOs, government agencies, and local communities that we can achieve sustainable development and create a prosperous future for all.

PROSPERITY PLAYBOOK: MASTERING WEALTH CREATION
& MANAGEMENT FOR THE MODERN INVESTOR

7. PERSONAL DEVELOPMENT FOR FINANCIAL SUCCESS

Personal development plays a pivotal role in achieving financial success. It encompasses a deliberate and continuous effort to enhance our skills, knowledge, and mindset in order to reach our financial goals. By focusing on personal development, we can unlock our true potential and create a solid foundation for financial success.

1. Self-Reflection and Goal Setting:

Embark on your personal development journey by engaging in deep self-reflection. Take stock of your current financial situation and evaluate how it aligns with your values and aspirations. Identify your strengths, weaknesses, opportunities, and threats. This introspective exploration will provide valuable insight into areas for improvement and help you set clear, measurable financial goals. Write these goals down and create a comprehensive action plan to achieve them.

2. Enhancing Financial Literacy:

Financial success demands a solid understanding of basic financial concepts. Begin by educating yourself on topics such as budgeting, saving, investing, and managing debt. Read books by renowned financial experts, attend seminars, or take online courses to improve your financial literacy. This knowledge will empower you to make informed decisions and navigate the complex world of finance with confidence and competence.

Dive deep into the world of finance by understanding complex investment strategies, tax planning, and risk management. Educate yourself on different types of investments including stocks, bonds, real estate, and alternative investment vehicles. Explore different asset classes and diversification strategies to build a well-balanced investment portfolio. By continually expanding your financial knowledge, you will have the tools to make wise and informed decisions to grow and protect your wealth.

3. Developing Strong Money Management Habits:
Cultivate disciplined money management habits to ensure long-term financial success. Create a realistic budget that accounts for your income, expenses, savings, and investments. Prioritize saving by setting aside a portion of your income each month and diligently sticking to your savings plan. Avoid impulsive spending and unnecessary debt, finding contentment in financial prudence and delayed gratification. By mastering these habits, you can build a solid financial foundation that withstands unexpected challenges.

Furthermore, focus on developing your ability to manage debt effectively. Explore options for consolidating high-interest debts and create a repayment plan that fits your financial circumstances. Paying down debts strategically will not only improve your financial health but also increase your credit score, opening doors to favorable interest rates and financial opportunities.

4. Continuous Learning and Skill Development:
Embrace a lifelong commitment to learning and personal growth. Constantly seek opportunities to acquire new skills

and knowledge that are relevant to your financial goals. Identify skills in areas such as negotiation, entrepreneurship, marketing, or financial analysis and take proactive steps to develop them. Attend workshops, enroll in courses, seek mentorship, or explore online learning platforms. By expanding your skills and knowledge, you create abundant opportunities to increase your income and build wealth.

In addition to acquiring specialized skills, focus on developing essential interpersonal skills such as effective communication, networking, and leadership abilities. These skills will enhance your professional development and increase your chances of career advancement, financial growth, and lucrative opportunities.

5. Building Resilience and Overcoming Obstacles:

Financial success is rarely a linear journey. It demands resilience and the ability to overcome various obstacles. Focus on developing a growth mindset that embraces challenges as learning experiences and opportunities for growth. Cultivate emotional intelligence to effectively manage setbacks, maintaining a positive attitude and unwavering determination. Surround yourself with a support network that encourages and motivates you on your path to financial success. By building resilience, you can weather storms with grace and continue progressing towards your goals.

Additionally, take the time to assess and manage risk effectively. While taking calculated risks is essential for financial growth, it is important to evaluate the potential consequences and mitigate them to the best of your ability. Conduct thorough research, seek expert advice, and evaluate risk-reward ratios before stepping into new ventures or investment opportunities. By developing strong risk management skills, you can make informed decisions and minimize potential losses.

6. Mindset Shift: From Scarcity to Abundance:

Adopting an abundance mentality is crucial for achieving financial success. Let go of limiting beliefs about money and replace them with a mindset of abundance and prosperity. Believe in your innate ability to generate wealth and attract opportunities for financial growth. Practice gratitude for what you already have while maintaining clarity and focus on your financial goals. This shift in mindset will transform your perspective, enabling you to embrace abundance and attract more opportunities into your life.

To strengthen your abundance mindset, engage in visualization exercises, affirmations, and meditation. Visualize your financial goals as already achieved and cultivate a deep sense of gratitude for the opportunities and abundance in your life. Surround yourself with positive affirmations that reinforce your belief in abundance and your ability to attract wealth and success. By embracing an abundance mindset, you will become a magnet for financial opportunities and experiences.

7. Taking Calculated Risks and Embracing Failure:

Financial success often requires taking calculated risks and stepping outside your comfort zone. Be willing to explore opportunities that have the potential for high returns, carefully assessing the risks involved. Understand that failure is a natural part of the journey towards success. Embrace failure as a valuable learning experience and a stepping stone towards future achievements. Develop resilience and learn from each setback, adjusting your strategies along the way. The willingness to take risks and learn from both success and failure will greatly contribute to your financial growth.

Embracing failure also involves adopting a proactive approach to learn from mistakes and making necessary adjustments. Develop a growth mindset that views failure as an opportunity for growth rather than a setback. Analyze your failures objectively, identify the lessons learned, and use those insights to refine your strategies and decision-making processes. With every failure, you become stronger and more resilient, equipping yourself with the knowledge and experience to make better financial choices in the future.

8. Maintaining Balance and Well-being:

While financial success is a significant aspect of our lives, it is important to maintain balance and prioritize overall well-being. Nurture your physical health through regular exercise, adequate sleep, and a nutritious diet. Practice self-care, engage in activities that bring you joy, and recharge your energy levels. Cultivate meaningful relationships with family, friends, and mentors who support your personal and financial growth. Take time for personal reflection, introspection, and inner growth. A holistic approach to personal development will lead to long-term financial success and fulfillment in all aspects of life.

Additionally, prioritize your mental and emotional well-being. Engage in activities such as meditation, journaling, or therapy to manage stress, anxiety, and any negative emotions that may hinder your financial success. Develop a support system that includes mentors, coaches, or like-minded individuals who can provide guidance and accountability as you navigate your financial journey. Take breaks and engage in activities that rejuvenate your mind and provide clarity. By nurturing your overall well-being, you create a solid foundation for financial success and a fulfilling life.

By actively engaging in personal development, we can unlock our potential for financial success. Embrace this journey of continuous growth, learn from your experiences, and never stop striving for excellence. Your commitment to personal development is the key to unlocking your financial goals and living a prosperous and fulfilled life.

8. DIVERSIFYING YOUR INVESTMENT PORTFOLIO

Diversifying Your Investment Portfolio:

Diversification is a crucial aspect of successful investing as it helps spread risk and maximize potential returns. By allocating investments across different asset classes, sectors, geographic regions, and investment vehicles, investors can achieve a balanced portfolio that is less vulnerable to market volatility. In this extended chapter, we will delve deeper into the importance of diversification and explore various strategies to effectively diversify your investment portfolio.

1. Understanding the Benefits of Diversification:

Diversification plays a vital role in mitigating risk. Sudden market fluctuations or economic downturns can have a severe impact on specific asset classes or industries. By spreading investments across different asset classes such as stocks, bonds, real estate, commodities, and cash equivalents, investors can reduce the risk of losing their entire investment in a single asset. Each asset class possesses its own risk and return characteristics, and diversification allows for a balance between risk and reward.

2. Asset Class Diversification:

Investors should aim to diversify across various asset classes to achieve optimal portfolio diversification. Stocks provide long-term growth potential; however, they are more volatile compared to other asset classes. Bonds offer stability and generate income through interest payments, making them desirable for risk-averse investors. Real estate investments can offer both income and capital appreciation potential. Commodities, such as precious metals or agricultural products, add diversification benefits due to their lower correlation with traditional asset classes. Additionally, cash equivalents, including savings accounts and money market funds, provide liquidity and capital preservation. By diversifying across these asset classes, investors can potentially benefit from the varying performance cycles of different markets, reducing the overall risk of their portfolio.

3. Geographic Diversification:
Investing in different geographic regions is another significant aspect of diversification. Economic and political conditions can significantly impact markets and investments across countries. By having exposure to various economies, investors can protect their investments from country-specific risks. A globally diversified portfolio benefits from the growth potential of emerging markets while maintaining exposure to stable, developed economies. However, it is essential to consider factors such as regulatory environments, currency risks, and geopolitical stability when diversifying geographically.

4. Sector Diversification:

Diversifying across sectors or industries is crucial to minimize risks associated with individual sectors. Different sectors perform differently depending on market conditions. For instance, during an economic downturn, defensive sectors like healthcare or consumer staples tend to be more resilient, while cyclical sectors like technology and consumer discretionary may experience more significant fluctuations. By spreading investments across sectors, investors can reduce the impact of industry-specific risks and potential market volatility, balancing the overall risk of their portfolio. Thorough research and analysis of sectors should be conducted to assess their growth potential, competitive advantages, and regulatory risks.

5. Investment Vehicle Diversification:

Diversification can also be achieved by utilizing different investment vehicles. Mutual funds and exchange-traded funds (ETFs) enable investors to gain exposure to a diversified portfolio managed by professionals. These investment vehicles pool funds from multiple investors and invest in a broad range of assets, providing diversification within a single investment. In contrast, individual stocks allow investors to select specific companies directly, providing potential for higher returns but also higher risks. Combining investment vehicles can leverage their distinct advantages and contribute to effective portfolio diversification. Additionally, alternative investments like private equity, hedge funds, or venture capital offer further diversification opportunities, although they require thorough due diligence due to their relatively illiquid and high-risk nature.

6. Rebalancing and Monitoring:

Maintaining a diversified portfolio requires regular monitoring and rebalancing. Over time, certain investments may outperform others, causing imbalances in the portfolio's asset allocation. Periodically reassessing and rebalancing the portfolio ensures it remains aligned with investment goals and risk tolerance. Rebalancing involves selling overperforming assets and allocating more funds to underperforming ones. This disciplined approach prevents concentration in a particular asset class or sector and allows for a consistent risk and return profile. Factors such as transaction costs, tax implications, and long-term investment strategies should be considered during the rebalancing process.

7. Seeking Professional Advice:

Diversifying a portfolio can be complex, especially when considering various asset classes, sectors, and investment vehicles. Seeking advice from financial professionals can be invaluable, particularly in dealing with intricate investment options or assessing risk exposures. Financial advisors can provide insights, help tailor strategies to specific needs, and assist in navigating the ever-changing investment landscape. They can offer guidance on appropriate asset allocations, help identify suitable investment vehicles, and provide ongoing portfolio monitoring to ensure effective diversification.

In conclusion, diversification is a fundamental risk management tool for investors. By diversifying across asset classes, geographic regions, sectors, and investment vehicles, investors can reduce their exposure to unnecessary risks and increase their chances of achieving long-term financial success. Regularly reviewing and adjusting the portfolio based on investment goals, risk tolerance, and market conditions is crucial for maintaining an optimized and diversified portfolio. Remember, diversification does not guarantee profits or protect against losses, but when implemented strategically, it can provide stability and improved risk-adjusted returns.

9. THE ROLE OF STARTUPS IN WEALTH CREATION

Startups have emerged as dynamic and transformative players in the modern economy, reshaping industries and opening new pathways for wealth creation. Their impact is evident in the way they stimulate innovation, spur economic growth, and generate employment opportunities. In this extended chapter, we will delve deeper into the multifaceted ways startups contribute to wealth creation and elucidate their potential benefits for investors and society at large.

At the heart of startup success lies their ability to introduce disruptive ideas and technologies to market. These fledgling ventures often identify gaps or flaws in existing industries and offer innovative solutions that create value for customers. By challenging the status quo and introducing fresh perspectives, startups unlock previously untapped markets and create new avenues for generating wealth.

Notably, startups possess an inherent agility and adaptability. They can swiftly pivot their strategies and business models in response to market feedback, capitalizing on emerging opportunities and maneuvering through change more effectively than established corporations. This nimbleness equips startups with the potential for rapid growth and the ability to generate substantial returns for their investors.

Furthermore, startups are typically at the forefront of technological advancements, embracing cutting-edge technologies and harnessing their power to disrupt established industries. This not only generates wealth for the startup itself but also triggers a ripple effect in the broader economy. Innovation spillovers occur when startups develop new technologies, processes, or business models that are subsequently adopted by other companies, resulting in a surge of economic growth and fresh avenues for wealth creation.

The impact of startups on job creation cannot be understated. As these ventures expand, they require a skilled workforce to support their operations, leading to the creation of new employment opportunities. This influx of jobs not only stimulates economic activity but also enhances overall prosperity. Moreover, startups foster a culture of talent development and entrepreneurial spirit, attracting ambitious individuals who are driven to create value and contribute to the economy.

Startups also have the potential to address societal challenges while generating wealth. Many startups are focused on tackling pressing issues such as sustainability, healthcare, education, and social inequalities. By developing innovative solutions to address these challenges, startups not only create wealth but also contribute to the welfare of society as a whole. Their solutions often have far-reaching positive impacts, improving living standards, promoting equality, and creating opportunities for underrepresented communities.

For those seeking higher returns on their investments, startups offer an enticing opportunity. Although investing in startups entails higher risks compared to established companies, the potential rewards are equally substantial. Successful investments in startups can yield significant financial gains, as these ventures often experience exponential growth and attract lucrative acquisitions or initial public offerings (IPOs).

Beyond financial benefits, investing in startups often enables individuals to actively engage in the growth journey of the company. This level of involvement can bring not only monetary rewards but also a sense of fulfillment and satisfaction, knowing that one has contributed to the success of a promising venture. Investors can leverage their experience, expertise, and networks to support startups, creating a symbiotic relationship where both parties benefit.

To foster long-term prosperity and harness the potential for wealth creation, it is crucial to develop a supportive ecosystem for startups and make strategic investments in these ventures. By providing mentorship, access to capital, and conducive regulatory environments, individuals and societies can fuel the growth and impact of startups, further leveraging their potential for innovation, market disruption, and wealth creation.

Governments play a vital role in creating an enabling environment for startups to thrive. By implementing policies that reduce red tape, streamline regulatory processes, and provide tax incentives, governments can attract entrepreneurship and encourage startup formation. Additionally, governments can invest in infrastructure, research and development, and education to cultivate a skilled workforce and foster innovation.

Collaboration between startups and established corporations can also drive wealth creation. Through partnerships, established companies can reap the benefits of startup innovation while startups gain access to resources, expertise, and market reach. These collaborations can lead to the development of groundbreaking products and services, opening up new revenue streams and accelerating wealth creation for both parties.

In conclusion, startups represent dynamic catalysts for wealth creation, propelling innovation, creating new markets, and generating employment opportunities. Their agility, focus on technological advancements, disruptive mindset, and potential to address societal challenges make them formidable agents of change in the global economy. By nurturing a conducive environment for startups, making targeted investments, and fostering collaboration, individuals, governments, and corporations can unlock the immense potential for wealth creation, ultimately fostering enduring prosperity.

PROSPERITY PLAYBOOK: MASTERING WEALTH CREATION
& MANAGEMENT FOR THE MODERN INVESTOR

———

10. THE POWER OF COMPOUND INTEREST

Compound interest is a phenomenon that has the potential to transform your financial future. Its compounding effect allows your money to grow not only on the initial investment but also on the accumulated interest from previous periods. In essence, it's like a snowball rolling down a hill, gathering momentum and size as it progresses. Understanding and harnessing the power of compound interest can be the key to unlocking financial success.

To grasp the true magnitude of compound interest, let's delve deeper into the mechanics of how it works. At its core, compound interest is calculated based on three key factors: the principal amount, the interest rate, and the time period. The principal amount refers to the initial investment, while the interest rate determines how much interest is earned on the principal. The time period represents how long the investment is allowed to compound.

There are two types of compound interest: annually or more frequently compounded interest. Annually compounded interest is calculated and added to the principal once a year, while more frequent compounding occurs quarterly, monthly, or even daily. The more frequently compounding occurs, the greater the effect on your investment growth.

To illustrate the power of compound interest, let's consider a hypothetical example. You start with an initial investment of $10,000 and invest it in a savings account with an annual interest rate of 8%. In the first year, you would earn $800 in interest, resulting in a total investment of $10,800. If the interest is compounded annually, the total investment remains the same throughout subsequent years. However, with more frequent compounding, your investment potential multiplies.

Suppose the interest is compounded annually for the first year and then switches to quarterly compounding for the subsequent years. By the end of the second year, you would have accumulated $10,816, just slightly more than with annual compounding. However, by the end of the fifth year, the power of quarterly compounding becomes evident, with your investment growing to $11,695. Comparatively, annually compounded interest would only grow your investment to $11,467, showcasing the substantial advantage of more frequent compounding.

Now, let's explore the concept of compound interest in the context of different investments. While a traditional savings account provides a safe and stable option, the returns are typically modest. However, other investment vehicles, such as stocks, bonds, mutual funds, and retirement accounts, offer the potential for higher returns and compounded growth.

Investing in the stock market, for example, has historically outperformed other investment options over the long haul, despite its inherent volatility. By investing in a diversified portfolio of stocks, you can increase your chances of achieving compounding growth. It is important to note that while investing in stocks can yield significant returns, it also carries a higher level of risk compared to more conservative options.

Bonds are another investment vehicle where compound interest plays a crucial role. When you purchase a bond, you essentially lend money to a government or corporation in exchange for regular interest payments. These interest payments can be reinvested, compounding and steadily growing your investment over time.

Mutual funds, on the other hand, pool money from multiple investors to invest in a diversified portfolio of securities, such as stocks and bonds. The returns generated by the fund are reinvested, allowing your investment to compound over time. This combined growth potential, along with the professional management of the fund, can be advantageous for those seeking compound interest.

Additionally, there are specialized accounts dedicated to compounding growth. Certificates of Deposit (CDs) are a type of savings account that offers fixed interest rates over a specific period of time, typically ranging from a few months to several years. These accounts often have higher interest rates than regular savings accounts, and the interest can compound depending on the terms of the CD.

Lastly, retirement accounts, such as 401(k)s and IRAs, offer a tax-advantaged way to maximize the power of compound interest. By contributing to these accounts, you can take advantage of tax-deferral or tax-free growth. This means that not only will your contributions compound over time, but the taxes on your investment growth are deferred or eliminated, allowing your money to grow even faster.

It is essential to understand that compound interest is not a magic bullet for instant wealth. It requires patience, discipline, and a long-term perspective. It is a gradual process that builds momentum over time, growing your wealth in a measured and sustainable way.

To ensure you make the most of compound interest, here are a few key strategies to
consider:

1. Start investing early: The power of compound interest is amplified the longer your money is allowed to grow. Starting early gives you a significant advantage in achieving your financial goals. The compounding effect becomes more powerful with each year that passes.

2. Stay invested for the long term: Avoid the temptation to constantly switch investments or withdraw funds prematurely. Compound interest thrives on consistent long-term investments. The longer you stay invested, the greater the potential for your money to compound and grow.

3. Maximize contributions to retirement accounts: Take advantage of tax-advantaged retirement accounts to accelerate your compound growth. Maximize your contributions and benefit from tax deferral or tax-free growth. Contribute the maximum amount allowed each year to make the most of this powerful tool.

4. Diversify your portfolio: Spreading your investments across different asset classes and industries can minimize risk and optimize compound growth potential. A well-diversified portfolio is key to long-term wealth accumulation. Consider diversifying across stocks, bonds, real estate, and other asset classes to mitigate risk and capture different growth opportunities.

5. Reinvest dividends and interest: Whenever possible, reinvest the interest or dividend payments you receive. By reinvesting these earnings, you allow compound interest to work its magic and accelerate your investment growth.

Reinvesting ensures that your returns are compounding and compounding upon themselves, leading to exponential growth over time.

6. Keep an eye on fees: Pay attention to the fees associated with your investments as they can eat into your compound growth over time. High fees, especially in actively managed funds, can significantly impact your overall returns. Evaluate the fees and expenses involved when choosing investment vehicles to make informed decisions.

In conclusion, compound interest has the power to transform your financial trajectory. It is a force that, when harnessed correctly, can propel your wealth to new heights. By understanding how compound interest functions, exploring various investment opportunities, and implementing sound financial strategies, you can unlock the full potential of compound interest and pave the way to a brighter financial future. Remember, the key is to start early, stay invested for the long term, diversify your portfolio, and reinvest your earnings. The power to grow your wealth through compound interest lies in your hands.

PROSPERITY PLAYBOOK: MASTERING WEALTH CREATION
& MANAGEMENT FOR THE MODERN INVESTOR

11. CASE STUDY: RAY DALIO'S INVESTMENT PHILOSOPHY

In this chapter, we will delve into the intriguing investment philosophy of one of the most successful investors of our time - Ray Dalio. Dalio is the founder of Bridgewater Associates, one of the world's largest hedge funds.

Dalio's investment philosophy is rooted in the concept of "radical transparency" and "thoughtful disagreement." He believes that by encouraging open and honest discussions, better investment decisions can be made. This philosophy has been instrumental in Bridgewater's success.

One of the key principles that Dalio advocates is diversification. He firmly believes in building a portfolio that is diversified across different asset classes and geographical regions. Dalio understands that the investment landscape is ever-changing and that different market conditions affect various assets differently. By spreading investments across a variety of asset classes, such as stocks, bonds, commodities, and even currencies, he aims to reduce the overall risk of the portfolio. This helps to mitigate potential losses in times of market downturns while allowing for the potential upside of different assets to capture market growth.

Furthermore, Dalio's approach to diversification is based on extensive research and data analysis, which enables him to make informed decisions. Bridgewater Associates has developed sophisticated computer algorithms and models that analyze vast amounts of data to identify patterns and trends within the market. By using this systematic approach, Dalio can identify correlations, outliers, and potential risks in investment opportunities. It allows him to identify areas that would benefit his diversified portfolio and act on them accordingly.

Another aspect of Dalio's investment philosophy is his focus on understanding the broader economic landscape and market cycles. He emphasizes the importance of studying historical patterns and economic indicators to predict market trends. By analyzing past market cycles, he can identify potential turning points and invest accordingly. For instance, when signs of economic growth appear, Dalio may increase exposure to equities and other growth-oriented assets. Conversely, during periods of economic downturn or uncertainty, he may shift towards more defensive assets such as bonds or cash to preserve capital.

Dalio also places great importance on risk management. He believes that understanding and managing risks are crucial for long-term investment success. He employs a systematic approach to risk management, incorporating risk-reward trade-offs in his investment strategies. This involves defining and quantifying risks, setting risk limits, and implementing risk mitigation strategies. Dalio understands that no investment is without risk, but by managing and balancing risk exposures, he seeks to achieve consistent returns over the long run.

Furthermore, Dalio's philosophy embraces the concept of embracing mistakes and failures as opportunities for growth and learning. He believes that reflecting on past mistakes allows him to continuously improve his investment strategies. Bridgewater has a unique approach to this, where employees are encouraged to openly discuss and share their mistakes and learnings as part of the investment process. By fostering an environment of open communication and learning from mistakes, Dalio creates an environment that promotes growth and innovation, leading to more successful investment outcomes.

When it comes to the implementation of his investment philosophy, Dalio employs a systematic approach that relies heavily on data analysis and decision-making frameworks. His famous "Principles" outline his overarching approach to decision-making and provide a guide to understanding how he thinks about the market. These principles include concepts such as "believability-weighted decision-making," which involves assigning higher weights to individuals or sources of information with proven track records of success.

Additionally, Dalio's investment philosophy incorporates the concept of "meaningful work" into his decision-making process. He believes that meaningful work and personal fulfillment lead to innovation and success. By aligning his investments with sectors and companies that have a positive impact on society, Dalio aims to create both financial returns and positive change.

In terms of Bridgewater Associates' investment process, Dalio emphasizes the importance of creating a strong culture within the organization. He believes that a cohesive and collaborative team is critical to making successful investment decisions. This culture is built on honest and direct feedback, where employees are expected to challenge each other's ideas in a respectful manner. By fostering an environment where diverse opinions are valued, Dalio ensures that the best ideas are considered and implemented.

Moreover, Dalio's focus on continuous learning and improvement is embedded in his investment process. He emphasizes the importance of rigorous analysis and testing of investment ideas, encouraging his team to actively seek feedback and critique their work. This iterative approach allows for constant refinement of investment strategies and decision-making frameworks.

Throughout this chapter, we have explored real-life case studies based on Dalio's investment philosophy, showcasing how his principles have contributed to his successful investment track record. These case studies have provided valuable insights and practical tips for investors looking to apply a similar approach to their own investment portfolios.

In conclusion, Ray Dalio's investment philosophy is a remarkable example of how a thoughtful and data-driven approach can lead to long-term investment success. By incorporating principles such as diversification, risk management, and embracing mistakes, investors can navigate the complex financial landscape with confidence. Dalio's emphasis on research, data analysis, and understanding of market cycles provides a robust framework for making informed investment decisions. This case study serves as an inspiration for those looking to build their wealth and achieve financial prosperity by employing a systematic and disciplined investment approach.

12. THE PSYCHOLOGY OF WEALTH MANAGEMENT

Understanding the psychology behind wealth management is crucial for achieving long term financial success. It is not just about numbers and strategies; it is about understanding our thoughts, emotions, and behaviors around money.

1. The Money Mindset:

Developing a healthy money mindset is the foundation of effective wealth management. Our thoughts and beliefs about money can significantly impact our financial decisions and actions. It is important to identify any negative or limiting beliefs we may have and work on reframing them into positive and empowering beliefs.

Cultivating a money mindset involves examining our attitudes towards wealth and abundance. One common belief that can hold us back is the scarcity mindset, where we believe that there is limited wealth and resources available to us. This mindset often leads to fear, hoarding, and a reluctance to take risks. By shifting our perception to an abundance mindset, we begin to see opportunities and believe that there is enough wealth to go around. This mindset encourages us to think creatively, take calculated risks, and seek out wealth-building opportunities.

Additionally, a money mindset involves understanding the

role of money in our lives. Money is a tool that can help us achieve our goals, provide security and freedom, and make a positive impact on society. By viewing money as a means to create value and fulfill our purpose, we can cultivate a healthier relationship with wealth.

To develop and strengthen our money mindset, it can be helpful to engage in practices such as visualization, affirmations, and gratitude. Visualizing our financial success and repeatedly affirming positive beliefs about money can rewire our subconscious mind and shift our behavior towards wealth-building actions. Expressing gratitude for the money and abundance we already have creates a sense of abundance and attracts more opportunities for financial growth.

2. Emotional Intelligence:
Emotions play a significant role in our financial decisions. Managing emotions effectively can prevent impulsive and irrational decisions that may lead to financial losses. Developing emotional intelligence involves understanding and regulating our emotions, as well as being aware of the impact emotions can have on our decision-making process.

Emotional intelligence begins with self-awareness. Recognizing our emotional triggers and understanding how they influence our financial behavior is essential. For example, recognizing that fear may lead us to sell investments prematurely during market downturns helps us make more rational decisions based on long-term goals rather than short-term fluctuations.

Cultivating emotional resilience allows us to navigate market volatility and make rational decisions, even during times of uncertainty. This resilience involves acknowledging and accepting our emotions without being overwhelmed by them. It means understanding that emotions are natural responses to events but making a conscious effort to separate them from our financial decisions.

Furthermore, practicing empathy can help us manage relationships and conflicts related to money. Understanding the emotions and perspectives of others, especially when making financial decisions with partners or family members, can lead to more effective communication and collaboration. Open and honest discussions about shared financial goals, fears, and aspirations can foster a sense of unity and support in wealth management.

3. Avoiding Cognitive Biases:

Cognitive biases are inherent flaws in our thinking that can lead to irrational decision making. Being aware of common biases such as confirmation bias, loss aversion, and overconfidence can help us make more rational financial decisions. It is important to challenge our own biases and seek objective information when making investment choices.

Confirmation bias refers to our tendency to seek out information that confirms our pre-existing beliefs while ignoring or dismissing contradictory evidence. To overcome this bias, we need to actively seek out diverse viewpoints and consider alternative perspectives. Engaging in critical thinking and conducting thorough research can help us make well informed decisions based on evidence and data.

Loss aversion is another common bias that leads us to fear losses more than we value gains. This bias can result in missed investment opportunities or premature selling of investments due to fear of potential losses. By focusing on long-term goals and staying balanced in our approach, we can better manage this bias and make decisions based on our overall investment strategy.

Overconfidence bias is the tendency to overestimate

our abilities and underestimate risks. While confidence is beneficial, it is important to stay humble and realistic when making financial decisions. Seeking feedback and advice from trusted professionals can provide a more objective perspective and help us avoid costly mistakes.

4. Setting Realistic Goals:

Setting clear and realistic financial goals is essential for wealth management. Goals provide direction and motivation, and they help us measure our progress. It is important to set both short-term and long-term goals and regularly review and adjust them as needed. Having a sense of purpose and a clear vision of what we want to achieve with wealth can help guide our financial decisions.

When setting goals, it is crucial to align them with our values and priorities. Reflecting on what truly matters to us, whether it's providing for loved ones, pursuing meaningful experiences, or making a positive impact on society, allows us to create goals that are personally fulfilling.

Additionally, breaking down long-term goals into smaller, achievable milestones helps us maintain focus and celebrate our progress along the way. Regularly reviewing and reassessing our goals ensures that they remain relevant and adaptable to changes in our lives.

Alongside setting goals, it is important to establish a comprehensive financial plan that includes strategies for saving, investing, managing debt, and budgeting. A well-thought-out plan provides a roadmap for wealth management and increases the likelihood of achieving financial success.

5. Building Discipline and Patience:

Wealth management requires discipline and patience. It is important to create a financial plan and stick to it, even in the face of temptations and market fluctuations. Avoiding impulsive decisions and staying committed to the long-term plan can lead to greater financial stability and growth.

Developing discipline involves creating routines and habits that support our financial goals. This can include automating savings and investing, practicing mindful spending, and regularly monitoring our progress. Delayed gratification is also a key aspect of building discipline; being willing to forego immediate pleasures for future financial security and well being.

Cultivating patience is equally important. Wealth accumulation is a gradual process that requires time and consistent effort. Understanding that short-term fluctuations are normal and focusing on long-term goals helps us avoid making hasty decisions based on fear or greed.

Patience also involves staying informed and educated about investment strategies and economic trends. Keeping up with financial news, attending educational seminars, and engaging in continuous learning enhance our ability to make informed decisions and adapt to changing market conditions.

6. Seeking Professional Help:

Managing wealth can be complex, and seeking the assistance of financial professionals can be beneficial. Financial advisors, portfolio managers, tax experts, and estate planners can provide expertise, guidance, and objective perspectives that can help us make informed decisions. However, it is important to choose professionals carefully and ensure that they align with our values and goals.

When seeking professional help, it is crucial to ask questions, understand their approach to investing, and clarify any fees or conflicts of interest. A trusted advisor will prioritize our best interests and work collaboratively to create a customized plan that aligns with our financial goals, risk tolerance, and values.

Additionally, staying educated and informed about financial matters empowers us to have more meaningful conversations with professionals. Continuously learning about investment strategies, tax planning, and other relevant topics enhances our ability to make informed decisions and actively participate in the management of our wealth.

7. Practicing Gratitude and Giving BackPracticing gratitude and giving back are important aspects of wealth management. Expressing gratitude for the wealth and abundance we have attracts more positivity and helps us appreciate what we already have. It shifts our focus from what we lack to what we have, cultivating a sense of contentment and fulfillment.

Giving back not only helps make a positive impact on society but also brings a sense of purpose and fulfillment. Whether through charitable donations, volunteering, or supporting causes we believe in, giving back allows us to use our wealth to make a difference in the lives of others. It can also help us gain perspective on the role of money in our lives, reinforcing the idea that wealth is a means to create value and contribute to the greater good.
Furthermore, incorporating philanthropy into our wealth management plan can have tax benefits and help with estate planning. Working with professionals who specialize in philanthropy and legacy planning can provide guidance on how to structure charitable giving in a way that aligns with our values and financial goals.

It is important to note that wealth management is not just about accumulating wealth, but also about using it responsibly and consciously. Embracing a holistic approach to wealth management that takes into account our mindset, emotions, behaviors, and values can lead to sustainable financial success and a more fulfilling life.

PROSPERITY PLAYBOOK: MASTERING WEALTH CREATION
& MANAGEMENT FOR THE MODERN INVESTOR

———————

13. RISK MANAGEMENT IN INVESTING

In the world of investing, risk is an inevitable companion. Whether you are a seasoned investor or just starting out, understanding and managing risk is crucial for long-term success. In this chapter, we will explore various strategies and principles of risk management in investing, delving deeper into the topic to provide you with a comprehensive understanding of how to effectively navigate the uncertainties of the financial markets.

1. Diversification: One of the most effective ways to manage risk is through diversification. By spreading your investments across different asset classes, industries, and geographic regions, you can mitigate the impact of any single investment on your overall portfolio. Diversification eliminates the risk of having all your eggs in one basket and helps to reduce the likelihood of substantial losses. It is important to note that diversification does not guarantee a profit or protect against losses, especially during market downturns where most asset classes may be negatively affected.

2. Asset allocation: Asset allocation is the process of determining how your investment portfolio should be distributed across different asset classes, such as stocks, bonds, cash, and alternative investments. Strategic asset allocation involves setting a target allocation for each asset

class based on your risk tolerance, return objectives, and time horizon. By allocating your investments wisely, you can manage risk by balancing the potential for returns with the amount of risk you are willing to take on. It is crucial to periodically review and rebalance your asset allocation to maintain your desired risk level as market conditions and your investment goals evolve.

3. Risk assessment: Before making any investment, it is essential to assess the risk associated with the investment opportunity. This involves evaluating factors such as the investment's historical performance, market conditions, industry trends, and the overall economic landscape. Conducting thorough research and analysis can help you gain a better understanding of the potential risks and rewards of an investment. It is advisable to seek professional advice or consult experts in specific investment areas when evaluating complex or unfamiliar investments.

4. Risk tolerance: Understanding your risk tolerance is a fundamental aspect of risk management. Risk tolerance is the level of uncertainty or potential loss you are comfortable with when making investment decisions. Your risk tolerance can be influenced by various factors such as financial goals, time horizon, investment knowledge, and personal circumstances. It is essential to be honest with yourself about your risk tolerance to ensure that your investment decisions align with your comfort level. A mismatch between your risk tolerance and actual investments can lead to emotional decision-making during market fluctuations, potentially resulting in poor investment outcomes.

5. Stop-loss orders and protective strategies: A stop-loss order is an important risk management tool that allows you to automatically sell a security when it reaches a predetermined price. This strategy helps to limit potential losses by ensuring

that you exit a position before the price drops too much. Implementing protective strategies, such as buying put options or using trailing stops, can also provide downside protection during periods of market volatility. Although these tools can help manage risk, it is important to carefully consider their costs and potential impact on overall portfolio returns.

6. Regular portfolio review: Regularly reviewing your investment portfolio is essential for effective risk management. By assessing the performance of your investments, you can identify any underperforming assets and decide whether to reallocate your investments to better opportunities. This active management allows you to adjust your portfolio in response to changing market conditions and manage risk effectively. Additionally, it is crucial to periodically assess the overall risk level of your portfolio to ensure it aligns with your risk tolerance and investment goals.

7. Risk management in different asset classes:

a. Stocks: Stocks are an integral part of many investment portfolios, but they come with their own set of risks. Market volatility and company-specific risks, such as poor management decisions or regulatory changes, can impact stock prices. To manage stock market risk, it is crucial to conduct thorough research, diversify your holdings, and be prepared for both short-term fluctuations and long-term investment horizons.

b. Bonds: Bonds are considered relatively safer compared to stocks, but they still carry risks. Interest rate risk, credit risk, and inflation risk are factors that affect bond prices. To manage bond market risk, you can diversify across different issuers and maturities, consider investing in bond funds, and monitor interest rate movements.

c. Cash: While cash investments are generally considered low risk, they come with the risk of inflation eroding purchasing power over time. To manage this risk, it is important to strike a balance between holding enough cash for liquidity needs and investing in assets with potential for growth that can outpace inflation.

d. Alternative investments: Alternative investments, such as real estate, commodities, private equity, or hedge funds, offer potential diversification and return opportunities, but they also carry unique risks. These risks may include illiquidity, regulatory changes, valuation uncertainty, and operational risks. Conducting thorough due diligence and understanding the specific risks associated with each alternative investment is crucial for effective risk management.

8. Emotions and behavioral biases: Emotions and behavioral biases can often cloud rational decision-making when it comes to investing. Fear and greed are two common emotions that can lead investors to make impulsive decisions based on short-term market movements rather than long-term fundamentals. Behavioral biases, such as confirmation bias or loss aversion, can also influence investment decisions. Managing emotions and being aware of these biases is crucial for effective risk management. Developing a disciplined investment strategy, adhering to a long-term plan, and seeking objective advice can help counteract the influence of emotions and biases.

9. Financial education: Continuously educating yourself about different investment strategies, market dynamics, and risk management techniques is critical in becoming a successful investor. By staying informed and up to date with current trends and developments, you can make more informed decisions and effectively manage the risks

associated with investing. This may include reading books and articles, attending seminars or workshops, and engaging with investment professionals or online communities to gain insights and knowledge.

Remember, no investment is entirely risk-free. However, by implementing these risk management strategies and principles, you can minimize the impact of risk on your investment portfolio. Successful investing is about understanding and managing risks, making informed decisions, and maintaining a long-term perspective in line with your goals and risk tolerance. Through diligent research, careful planning, and disciplined execution, you can navigate the complexities of the financial markets and increase your chances of achieving your investment objectives.

14. CASE STUDY: SUCCESS STORIES FROM STARTUPS

Startups have been a driving force in the global economy, redefining industries and creating incredible wealth for their founders and investors. In this chapter, we will delve into some inspiring success stories from the world of startups, highlighting the key factors that contributed to their triumph. These stories serve as valuable lessons for aspiring entrepreneurs and investors alike.

One such notable success story is that of Airbnb. Started in 2008, by Brian Chesky, Joe Gebbia, and Nathan Blecharczyk, Airbnb revolutionized the hospitality industry by connecting homeowners with travelers looking for unique accommodation experiences. Initially faced with significant challenges and rejections, the founders persevered and found innovative ways to overcome obstacles. They launched the "Airbed and Breakfast" concept, targeting major events in need of additional lodging options. By offering affordable and unconventional spaces, such as air mattresses on living room floors, they provided a viable alternative to traditional hotels.

Recognizing the importance of trust and safety, Airbnb implemented several measures to alleviate concerns. They introduced a review system where hosts and guests could rate each other, enhancing transparency and accountability. Additionally, the company implemented verification processes, identity checks, and secure payment systems to protect both hosts and guests. These efforts significantly contributed to building confidence in the platform, enabling exponential growth.

As Airbnb expanded, it faced regulatory challenges and opposition from established players in the hotel industry. Local laws and zoning regulations presented obstacles that needed to be navigated. The company invested in public policy initiatives and built relationships with governments and communities to establish partnerships and demonstrate their commitment to responsible and sustainable hosting. Through these efforts, Airbnb successfully transformed an industry and continues to be one of the leaders in the global travel and hospitality market.

One key factor that contributed to Airbnb's success was its ability to tap into the sharing economy. By leveraging the excess capacity of people's homes, Airbnb created a marketplace where individuals could monetize their assets and travelers could have unique and personalized experiences. This disruptive business model not only provided an alternative to traditional accommodations but also empowered individuals to become entrepreneurs and generate income. The success of Airbnb demonstrated the potential of peer-to-peer sharing platforms and has inspired numerous similar startups across different industries.

Another success story that captured the essence of startup triumph is that of WhatsApp. Founded by Jan Koum and Brian Acton in 2009, WhatsApp aimed to provide a simple and secure messaging platform for users around the world. What set WhatsApp apart was its dedication to a clean and ad-free user experience, prioritizing user privacy and data security. The founders understood the power of word-of-mouth and focused on delivering a reliable, easy-to-use, and feature-rich messaging app.

WhatsApp's popularity skyrocketed as it provided a convenient alternative to traditional SMS and other messaging platforms. International users, especially in emerging markets, favored the app due to its low-cost messaging capabilities. The founders capitalized on this momentum by adopting a subscription-based model, charging a nominal fee after the first year of use. This approach allowed WhatsApp to monetize its massive user base while still offering a superior messaging experience.

In 2014, Facebook recognized the immense value and potential of WhatsApp and acquired the company for a staggering $19 billion. This acquisition provided WhatsApp with the necessary resources to expand its services and scale further while maintaining its core principles. Today, WhatsApp boasts over 2 billion monthly active users and remains one of the dominant messaging platforms globally.

The success of WhatsApp can be attributed to various factors. First and foremost, the founders' commitment to user experience and privacy built trust and loyalty among users. By providing a platform that was ad-free and focused on genuine connections, WhatsApp differentiated itself from its competitors. The ease of use and ability to exchange messages across different mobile operating systems further contributed to its widespread adoption.

Additionally, WhatsApp's strategic focus on emerging markets proved critical to its success. Recognizing that these markets had limited access to affordable communication services, WhatsApp filled a gap by offering messaging at low data costs. This approach allowed the company to build a massive user base, particularly in countries where traditional SMS rates were high. This focused expansion and targeted marketing efforts helped fuel WhatsApp's rapid growth.

Furthermore, we will explore the rise of Uber, a company that disrupted the traditional taxi industry worldwide. Founded by Travis Kalanick and Garrett Camp in 2009, Uber introduced a groundbreaking concept of ride-sharing, transforming the way people commute. Uber's success can be attributed to its relentless focus on customer experience, leveraging technology to offer convenience, affordability, and safety.

Uber understood that seamless user experience was paramount in its success. The app provided users with a simplified way to request rides, track their drivers' locations, and make cashless transactions. Seamless integration with GPS technology ensured accurate pickups and drop-offs, eliminating the frustrations often associated with traditional taxis.

To ensure passenger safety, Uber implemented rigorous driver screening processes, including criminal background checks and vehicle inspections. They also introduced features such as driver ratings, two-way feedback, and 24/7 customer support, enhancing trust and accountability within the platform. By prioritizing safety and reliability, Uber established itself as a credible alternative to traditional transportation services.

However, Uber faced significant regulatory hurdles and resistance from established taxi services in various markets. Traditional taxi drivers protested against Uber's disruption, leading to legal battles and regulatory challenges aimed at shutting down the service. Uber responded by engaging in public relations campaigns, mobilizing both its riders and drivers to advocate for their services. The company also sought partnerships with local governments and transit agencies, showcasing the potential for collaboration rather than competition.

Through these efforts, Uber not only weathered the storm but emerged as a dominant force in the transportation industry. Today, millions of riders across the globe rely on Uber for affordable and convenient transportation options.

The success of Uber can be attributed to its ability to identify and address pain points in the existing transportation system. By offering a seamless, technology-driven solution, Uber disrupted the traditional taxi industry, which was plagued by inefficiencies and poor customer experience. The convenience of on-demand transportation, real-time tracking, and upfront pricing resonated with consumers, resulting in rapid adoption.

Additionally, Uber's focus on innovation and continuous improvement helped it stay ahead of the competition. The company leveraged data analytics and machine learning to optimize driver allocation, reduce wait times, and enhance the overall user experience. By embracing emerging technologies and investing in research and development, Uber
positioned itself as a leader in the transportation industry.

Moreover, Uber's commitment to expanding its services beyond traditional taxis played a crucial role in its success. The introduction of UberX, UberPOOL, and other offerings catered to different customer preferences and increased the company's market reach. This diversification allowed Uber to tap into additional revenue streams and solidify its position as a comprehensive mobility platform.

In conclusion, these success stories from startups are a testament to the transformative power of entrepreneurship and the potential for exponential growth and wealth creation. By studying these case studies and learning from the strategies employed by successful startups, individuals can unlock their own potential for success in the dynamic and ever evolving world of startups. Whether it is identifying untapped market opportunities, building a strong brand, navigating through regulatory challenges, or prioritizing a superior user experience, these success stories provide a blueprint for aspiring entrepreneurs and investors to achieve their breakthroughs. The journeys of Airbnb, WhatsApp, and Uber exemplify the tenacity, innovation, and strategic thinking that shape startup success.

---

15. THE FUTURE OF INVESTING: TRENDS TO WATCH

As we approach a new era of investing, it is crucial to delve deeper into the emerging trends that will shape the financial landscape. In this extended chapter, we will explore the key trends to watch in the future of investing and their implications.

1. Technological Advancements: The advancements in technology have had a profound impact on the investing landscape, transforming the way investors access information, execute trades, and manage their portfolios. Artificial intelligence (AI) and machine learning algorithms have emerged as powerful tools for investment decision-making. These technologies analyze vast amounts of data, identify patterns, and generate insights that can help investors make more informed decisions. We can expect further advancements in AI driven investing tools and predictive analytics, empowering investors to navigate complex market dynamics with precision and agility.

2. Sustainable and Impact Investing: Sustainable and impact investing has gained significant momentum in recent years as investors increasingly prioritize environmental, social, and governance (ESG) factors. Under this approach, investors

not only seek financial returns but also aim to generate positive outcomes and address pressing global challenges. Beyond simply avoiding harmful investments, investors now actively seek opportunities to support companies and assets with measurable positive impacts. This trend has prompted the development of ESG metrics, standards, and reporting frameworks, providing investors with quantifiable data to make more sustainable investment decisions. As more investors align their investments with their values and impact preferences, the demand for ESG-focused products and services is likely to continue growing.

3. Alternative Investments: Investors are increasingly exploring alternative investments beyond traditional asset classes such as stocks and bonds. These alternatives, which include real estate, private equity, venture capital, hedge funds, and cryptocurrencies, offer diversification benefits and the potential for higher returns. However, investing in alternative assets requires specialized knowledge, due diligence, and risk management strategies to navigate their unique characteristics. Moreover, the regulatory environment surrounding these investments may vary, necessitating a sophisticated understanding of compliance requirements. As investors seek to diversify their portfolios and access new opportunities, alternative investments are likely to play a more significant role in the future of investing.

4. Globalization and Emerging Markets: Globalization has opened up investment opportunities beyond domestic markets. Emerging markets, in particular, present attractive prospects due to their high growth potential resulting from demographic shifts, rapid urbanization, and expanding consumer markets. Investing in emerging markets can provide diversification benefits and access to companies poised for growth. However, investing in these markets also comes with geopolitical risks, regulatory complexities,

and currency fluctuations. Investors must carefully evaluate and monitor these markets, leveraging insights from local expertise and partnering with experienced professionals to capture growth opportunities while effectively managing risks.

5. Personalized Investment Solutions: Technology has enabled the development of personalized investment solutions tailored to individual preferences, risk profiles, and financial goals. Robo-advisors, powered by sophisticated algorithms, offer automated portfolio management and investment advice, ensuring efficient and cost-effective solutions for smaller investors. Likewise, wealth management platforms provide access to a wide range of investment products and services. As technology continues to evolve, investors can expect more advanced solutions, such as personalized robo-advisors that integrate complex financial planning capabilities and enhance the quality and accessibility of automated investment management.

6. Changing Demographics: The emergence of millennials and Generation Z as the new investor demographic is significantly shaping the investment landscape. These generations have distinct preferences and priorities when it comes to investing. They prioritize sustainable investing, impact-driven approaches, and digital accessibility. As millennials and Gen Z accumulate more wealth in the coming years, their investment preferences and behaviors will have a profound impact on the strategies employed by companies and asset managers. This shift toward sustainable investment strategies is pushing companies to integrate environmental and social considerations into their core practices, leading to a broader emphasis on long-term value creation and responsible business practices.

7. Regulation and Compliance: The financial industry operates in a highly regulated environment, and investors must stay

abreast of changing regulations and compliance requirements. Governments and regulatory bodies continuously respond to evolving market dynamics, aiming to increase transparency, resilience, and investor protection. The proliferation of new investment products, strategies, and technology platforms has necessitated a more robust regulatory framework. Investors need to be aware of and comply with legal and regulatory frameworks, ensuring their investment practices align with industry standards. Staying informed about evolving regulations and partnering with trusted advisors can help investors navigate the complex landscape of compliance effectively.

8. Investor Education and Literacy: With the evolving investment landscape, there is an increasing need for investor education and financial literacy. Investors must have a solid understanding of different investment concepts, strategies, and risks to make informed decisions. As technology continues to reshape the industry, investors need to be knowledgeable about emerging trends, technological innovations, and regulatory changes. Financial literacy programs, online educational resources, and access to expert advice can empower investors to make sound investment decisions and navigate the future of investing effectively.

In conclusion, the future of investing presents exciting opportunities for investors who adapt and embrace emerging trends. Technological advancements, sustainable investing, alternative investments, globalization, personalized solutions, changing demographics, regulation, and investor education are the key factors shaping the investment landscape. By staying informed, being adaptable, and continually learning, investors can position themselves to thrive and achieve their financial goals in this ever-evolving environment.

16. THE ROLE OF NGOS IN WEALTH CREATION

NGOs, or non-governmental organizations, play a crucial and multifaceted role in creating wealth and promoting prosperity in societies around the world. While often associated with charitable work and humanitarian efforts, NGOs are also actively involved in socio economic development and empowerment initiatives, contributing to economic growth and improving the quality of life for individuals and communities.

One of the key ways in which NGOs contribute to wealth creation is through their focus on education and skill development programs. High-quality education is the cornerstone of socio-economic progress and a catalyst for individual empowerment. NGOs recognize the power of education in breaking the cycle of poverty and improving livelihoods. They work tirelessly to ensure that individuals, especially those in underprivileged communities, have access to quality education and vocational training. NGOs not only support formal education systems but also fill gaps by providing specialized training in fields such as information technology, entrepreneurship, and agricultural practices. Such targeted training equips individuals with the necessary knowledge and skills to participate meaningfully in the workforce, leading to increased employment opportunities, higher incomes, and overall prosperity.

In addition to education, NGOs support entrepreneurship and small-scale businesses, playing a significant role in fostering economic self-sufficiency. Through microfinance initiatives, NGOs provide financial resources to aspiring entrepreneurs who may not have access to traditional banking services. These initiatives not only offer microloans but also provide essential training and mentorship to help individuals develop their business acumen and managerial skills. By empowering individuals and communities to start their own businesses, NGOs create a ripple effect of job creation, economic activity, and poverty reduction. Moreover, these initiatives promote local economic development, reduce dependence on external aid, and contribute to sustainable livelihoods.

NGOs are instrumental in addressing economic inequality and advocating for inclusive development. They play a vital role in bridging the gap between marginalized communities and mainstream society. By working with governments, businesses, and other stakeholders, NGOs raise awareness about societal inequalities and advocate for policies that prioritize social welfare, equitable distribution of resources, and sustainable economic practices. They strive to ensure that marginalized communities have equal access to economic opportunities, financial services, and markets. NGOs also work towards removing barriers such as discriminatory practices, gender inequality, and social exclusion. Through their partnerships and collaborations, NGOs aim to create an environment where everyone has an equal opportunity to participate in and benefit from economic activities, thereby promoting a fair and just society.

Furthermore, NGOs recognize the interdependence between wealth creation and environmental sustainability. Many NGOs are actively involved in conservation efforts, promoting renewable energy solutions, and supporting communities in adopting sustainable farming and agricultural practices.

They work towards creating a balance between economic growth and environmental preservation. NGOs advocate for policies that encourage environmentally friendly practices within industries, promote green technologies, and invest in renewable energy sources. By recognizing the need to conserve natural resources and mitigate climate change, NGOs contribute to long-term economic stability and prosperity. They actively engage in environmental education and awareness programs to promote sustainable consumption and production patterns among individuals and communities.

While NGOs play a significant role in wealth creation, it is important to recognize that they cannot address all the challenges on their own. Collaboration between NGOs, governments, businesses, and individuals is crucial for sustainable development. This collaborative approach allows for the pooling of resources, expertise, and knowledge, leading to more effective and comprehensive solutions. By working together, different stakeholders can leverage their respective strengths and capacities to create lasting positive change in society.

In conclusion, NGOs have a multifaceted and vital role to play in wealth creation. Through their focus on education and skill development, support for entrepreneurship, advocacy for inclusive policies, and emphasis on sustainability, NGOs contribute to the holistic development of societies. They empower individuals, foster economic self-sufficiency, address inequality, and promote environmental stewardship. By working together with other stakeholders, we can harness the potential of NGOs and create a future where prosperity is accessible to all, and the well-being of both individuals and the planet is prioritized.

17. BUILDING A PROSPERITY MINDSET

Building a prosperity mindset is not just about positive thinking; it is about transforming your entire relationship with money, abundance, and success. It requires a deep understanding of the principles of wealth creation and a commitment to personal growth. In this extended version of the chapter, we will explore additional strategies that can help you develop a profound and lasting prosperity mindset.

9. Challenge Your Money Scripts: Money scripts are deep-seated beliefs and attitudes about money that we develop throughout our lives. These scripts often shape our financial behaviors and outcomes. Take the time to identify any negative or limiting money scripts you hold and replace them with empowering ones. For example, if you believe that "money is the root of all evil," shift your perspective to one that sees money as a tool for making a positive impact in the world.

10. Cultivate a Sense of Abundance: Many people operate from a scarcity mindset, believing that there is a limited amount of wealth and success to go around. To develop a prosperity mindset, you must embrace the concept of abundance. Recognize that there are infinite possibilities and opportunities available to you. Practice generosity and give back to others, as this promotes the flow of abundance into

your life.

11. Develop Financial Literacy: Expand your knowledge about personal finance and investment strategies. Educate yourself on topics such as budgeting, saving, investing, and understanding financial markets. By becoming financially literate, you gain the confidence and skills needed to make informed decisions and navigate the complex world of wealth creation.

12. Create Multiple Streams of Income: A prosperity mindset involves diversifying your sources of income. Relying solely on a single income stream can limit your financial growth. Explore different avenues for generating additional income, such as starting a side business, investing in rental properties, or exploring passive income opportunities like dividend paying stocks or royalties from intellectual property.

13. Embrace Delayed Gratification: Building wealth requires discipline and the ability to delay immediate pleasures for long-term gains. Practice delayed gratification by setting financial goals and consistently adhering to a saving and investment plan. Understand that sacrifices made today will pave the way for a more prosperous future.

14. Foster Resilience: Financial setbacks and challenges are inevitable on the path to building wealth. Developing resilience allows you to bounce back from setbacks and learn from failures. Embrace a growth mindset that sees failure as an opportunity for growth. Learn from your mistakes, adapt, and persevere, knowing that each setback brings you closer to success.

15. Align Your Financial Goals with Your Values: Clarify your core values and ensure your financial goals are aligned with them. When you are clear about what is truly important to you, your financial decisions will reflect those values. This alignment drives greater fulfillment and purpose in the

pursuit of wealth.

16. Practice Mindfulness: Incorporate mindfulness into your financial journey. Be fully present with your money, conscious of your spending habits, and aware of your emotions around money. By practicing mindfulness, you can make conscious financial decisions in alignment with your goals, rather than reacting impulsively or unconsciously.

17. Give Back and Make a Difference: Incorporate philanthropy into your prosperity mindset. When you have achieved financial success, consider how you can use your resources to make a positive impact on society. Giving back not only creates a sense of fulfillment but also attracts more abundance into your life.

18. Continuously Expand Your Financial Knowledge: Building a prosperity mindset requires a commitment to lifelong learning. Stay updated with industry trends, read books, attend seminars, and engage with mentors who can help you deepen your understanding of wealth creation strategies. By continuously expanding your financial knowledge, you enhance your ability to make informed decisions and seize opportunities.

19. Surround Yourself with Like-Minded Individuals: Surrounding yourself with people who share a prosperity mindset can be instrumental in your financial growth. Seek out individuals who inspire you, challenge you, and uplift you in your pursuit of abundance. Engage in mastermind groups, join professional associations, or attend networking events to connect with like-minded individuals who can support and amplify your journey.

20. Develop a Healthy Relationship with Risk: Building a prosperity mindset involves embracing calculated risks. Be willing to step outside your comfort zone and take intelligent

risks that have the potential for high rewards. By developing a healthy relationship with risk, you open yourself up to new opportunities and stretch your capacity for growth.

21. Practice Gratitude and Appreciation: Cultivating a sense of gratitude and appreciation for the abundance in your life is key to maintaining a prosperity mindset. Regularly reflect on and acknowledge the progress you have made, the resources at your disposal, and the opportunities that come your way. Gratitude amplifies positive emotions and attracts more reasons to be grateful.

22. Visualize and Affirm Your Desired Financial Reality: Visualization and affirmations are powerful tools to manifest your desired financial realities. Picture yourself living the life of abundance you envision, and affirm positive statements about your financial success. Engage all your senses in these visualizations and allow yourself to feel the emotions associated with achieving your goals. This practice helps align your subconscious mind with the prosperous future you desire.

By embracing these additional strategies, you deepen your understanding of building a prosperity mindset. Remember that true wealth encompasses more than just monetary abundance; it involves aligning your financial goals with your values, positively impacting others, and finding joy in the journey. With dedication, self-awareness, and a commitment to lifelong learning, you can cultivate a prosperity mindset that transcends mere financial success and leads to a life of fulfillment and purpose.

◆ ◆ ◆

18. CONCLUSION: YOUR PROSPERITY PLAYBOOK

In this final chapter, we will delve deeper into the key lessons and insights we have gained throughout this book. Creating wealth and achieving financial success is a long-term process that requires dedication, perseverance, and continuous learning. Let's explore an extended version of our prosperity playbook to provide you with a more comprehensive guide for navigating your financial goals.

1. Set Clear and SMART Goals:

Setting clear and SMART (Specific, Measurable, Achievable, Relevant, and Time-bound) goals is the foundation of your financial success. Begin by defining your long-term financial objectives, such as buying a house, starting a business, or retiring comfortably. Once you have determined your overarching goals, break them down into smaller, actionable steps and designate deadlines for each milestone. This approach will provide you with a clear roadmap to follow, making it easier to stay motivated and focused along the way.

Additionally, it is essential to review and reassess your goals periodically. As your circumstances change and new opportunities arise, you may need to adjust your goals accordingly. Flexibility and adaptability are crucial as you navigate the ever-changing landscape of wealth creation.

2. Develop a Wealth Mindset:

Cultivating a wealth mindset is an integral part of your long-term success. It involves adopting a positive and abundance-oriented outlook on life. To develop a wealth mindset, you must shift your beliefs and attitudes about money and abundance. Practice gratitude for what you have and what you will achieve. Utilize visualization techniques to imagine your financial success vividly. Surround yourself with individuals who support your wealth building journey and share a similar mindset. By embracing the power of positive thinking, you will attract opportunities and solutions that align with your financial goals.

3. Continuously Educate Yourself:

Building wealth requires a commitment to continuous learning. To stay ahead in the ever evolving world of finance and investments, you must invest in your knowledge and skills. Stay abreast of the latest investment strategies, economic trends, and business news. Attend industry conferences and seminars, take online courses, read books written by experts in the field, and follow thought leaders who have achieved the level of success you aspire to. Seek advice from trusted financial advisors and mentors who can guide you throughout your wealth-building journey. Remember, the more knowledge you acquire, the better-equipped you will be to make informed financial decisions.

4. Budget and Manage Expenses Wisely:

Creating and adhering to a budget is essential for financial success. A budget enables you to track your expenses and maintain control over your financial resources. Start by recording all your income and categorizing your expenses. Analyze your spending patterns and identify areas where you can reduce costs or eliminate non-essential expenses. Allocate a portion of your income towards saving and investing, making it a non-negotiable priority. As your income increases, resist the temptation to inflate your lifestyle and instead focus on expanding your assets, which appreciate in value over time. Regularly assess your budget and make necessary adjustments to ensure it aligns with your evolving financial goals.

5. Build Multiple Streams of Income:

Diversifying your income sources is crucial for financial stability and growth. Relying solely on a single income stream can be risky, particularly in today's volatile economy. Explore opportunities to create additional revenue streams that align with your skills, interests, and long-term goals. Consider starting a side business, investing in stocks or real estate, or taking on freelance projects. Building multiple streams of income not only provides a safety net against unexpected financial setbacks but also accelerates your wealth-building potential. However, it is essential to balance your time and resources effectively to ensure that each income stream receives adequate attention and nurturing.

6. Be Consistent in Saving and Investing:

Saving and investing should be an ongoing practice rather than a sporadic activity. Saving helps you build a financial cushion and create a foundation for investing. Make saving a habit by allocating a percentage of your income each month towards an emergency fund and other short-term savings goals. Automate the process when possible, so a portion of your paycheck is automatically directed to your savings or investment accounts. Compound interest and time are powerful allies when it comes to growing your wealth. As you accumulate savings, it is crucial to invest wisely to maximize your returns. Diversify your investment portfolio based on your risk tolerance and financial goals, ensuring you balance both short-term and long-term investments. Regularly review and rebalance your investments to stay aligned with your objectives and to address the changing market conditions.

7. Embrace Risk and Learn from Mistakes:

Building wealth often involves taking calculated risks. Stepping out of your comfort zone and embracing new opportunities can propel you towards financial success. While it is important to conduct thorough research and analysis before making any investment decisions, it is equally crucial to overcome the fear of failure. Understand that failure is not a destination but a valuable learning experience. Analyze your missteps, seek feedback from trusted advisors, and make adjustments accordingly. Each setback presents an opportunity for growth and improvement. By embracing risk and learning from your mistakes, you cultivate resilience and sharpen your decision-making skills, increasing your chances of achieving long-term financial prosperity.

8. Give Back to Society:

As you attain financial prosperity, remember the importance of giving back to society. Philanthropy offers a deeper sense of fulfillment and purpose beyond material gains. Identify causes and initiatives that align with your values and contribute to creating a more equitable society. Support charitable organizations or establish your own philanthropic ventures. Whether it is through financial contributions, volunteering your time and expertise, or leveraging your influence, use your wealth to make a positive impact on the world. Serving others and making a difference not only enriches the lives of those in need but also brings a greater sense of satisfaction and purpose to your own life.

By following these steps and adopting the principles outlined in this book, you will embark on a transformative journey towards creating sustainable wealth and achieving financial freedom. Remember, this journey is not a sprint but a marathon. Stay committed, stay focused, and never stop learning.

Congratulations on embarking on this rewarding path. Now, go out there and script your own success story. The world eagerly awaits the impact you will make.

BOOKS BY THIS AUTHOR

Naive Publishing

Discover the world of Naive Publishing, where we believe in the transformative power of words. Our diverse collection of titles is designed to inspire, educate, and entertain readers of all backgrounds and interests.

1. **Journeys of the Soul: A Guide to Transformative Travel** - Embark on a voyage of self-discovery with this all-encompassing guide. Embrace the unexpected, view challenges as opportunities for growth, and create lifelong memories along your journey.

2. **Living With Manic Depression** - A comprehensive guide for individuals and families navigating the complexities of bipolar disorder.

3. **The Serious Side to Humour: Strategies for Addressing Emotive Topics** - Discover how humor can be used as a tool to navigate challenging situations and foster empathy and understanding when addressing personal and societal struggles.

4. **Living in a Postcolonial World: Voices of Marginalised Communities** - Explore the experiences and perspectives of marginalized voices from former colonies, challenging the dominant narratives constructed by colonial powers.

5. **Purrfect Pixels: The Unraveling Love For Cats In The Digital

Age And Beyond** - Immerse yourself in the captivating world of cats and discover the timeless charm, wisdom, and love they bring to our lives.

6. **Unveiling 'The Exorcist': The Battle Of Good And Evil In William Peter Blatty's Masterpiece** - Delve into the chilling world of 'The Exorcist' with this comprehensive analysis of the iconic horror novel and its cultural impact.

7. **Napoleon: A Comprehensive Biography of a Military and Political Genius** - Coming soon!

8. **The Power Of Personal Growth: A Guide To Unlocking Your Potential And Achieving Success** - Coming soon!

9. **Niccolò Machiavelli: The Life and Legacy of a Renaissance Philosopher and Political Theorist** - Coming soon!

10. **Marketing Your Young Adult Graphic Novel: Strategies for Success** - Coming soon!

11. **The Ultimate Cookbook: 150 Recipes, Tips, And Techniques For Mastering The Kitchen** - Coming soon!

12. **Unveiling Panem's Dark Realities: Suzanne Collins' Dystopian Masterpiece** - Coming soon!

13. **Embracing The Magic: A Journey To Pleasure, Freedom, And Love** - Coming soon!

14. **My Nutritional Journey: A Guide to Dieting with Healthy Recipes (The Concise Nutrition and Lifestyle Guide)** - Coming soon!

At Naive Publishing, we are committed to delivering high-quality content that resonates with our readers. Our books are not just about the topics they cover; they are about the journey of self-discovery and personal growth that reading can inspire. Whether you're planning a trip, navigating personal struggles, or simply looking for a captivating read, Naive Publishing has the perfect book for you.

Discover the world of Naive Publishing today and let our books guide you on your path to transformative reading.